10 Ways to Make It Great!

Kristina,

You Make it GREAT!!

LCO 2009

10 Ways to Make It Great!

Phil Gerbyshak

2006

Advance Praise for 10 Ways to Make It Great!

"Phil absolutely owns the word 'great.' His expertise and experience have more than validated his authority in the self-improvement field. When you read his book, you will learn how to make improvements in your life, both large and small; both immediate and long term."

— Scott Ginsberg, author of HELLO my name is Scott & The Power of Approachability, professional speaker and "That Guy with the Nametag"

"This is not a book. Not in the traditional sense you may think of. What Phil Gerbyshak has created for us is a workbook, or more concisely, a Work it! book, so we can make something great happen in our lives. So we can be catalysts. Are you up for that challenge? If you are a passive reader, this is not for you; then again, neither is greatness."

— Rosa Say, founder and head coach of Say Leadership Coaching, and author of Managing with Aloha, Bringing Hawaii's Universal Values to the Art of Business

"Phil Gerbyshak is terminally upbeat. I don't know how he does it...well, actually now I do know. 10 Ways To Make It Great! details Phil's secrets and recommendations for transforming your outlook on life. This is a book filled with practical advice for breaking past plateaus and making real progress whether at home or at work."

— Brendon Connelly, author, SlackerManager.com

"I've always believed that great days lead to great weeks. Great weeks lead to great months. Great months lead to great quarters and great quarters lead to great years. If you fancy yourself as a Next Generation Leader and want to say one day that you've had a great career, invest some time with Phil Gerbyshak now, understanding how to make every day great."

— Rebecca Ryan, founder, Next Generation Consulting

"10 Ways to Make It Great! urges you to do two things: make a conscious choice for greatness, and get proactive. Reading Phil's book will leave you making new choices, and will provide you with specific proactive steps you can take to make today, tomorrow, and everyday. . . GREAT!"

—Kevin Eikenberry, Chief Potential Officer, speaker and author of Vantagepoints on Learning and Life

"Phil loads 10 Ways to Make It Great! with a plethora of practical insights and easy to take steps that will help anyone take their first step, or more steps towards growth and Greatness!"

– Kirk Weisler, Chief Morale Officer, Team Dynamics, Inc.

"Verb. Verb. Verb! 10 Ways to Make It Great! is a book of action. Phil's ten lessons for making it great transcend the noun of philosophy. Get it, live it and 'Make It Great!'"

– David E. Rothacker, author, Rothacker Reviews

"As a Life Purpose and Career Coach, I'm always interested in new ideas to support my clients in getting from where they are to where they want to go. Phil Gerbyshak's book 10 Ways To Make It Great! is chock-full of innovative ideas and resources for doing just that. Using his warm and conversational style, Phil encourages readers to take charge of their own lives in whichever areas they see opportunities to go beyond their own status quo. He challenges them to figure out what they really want, and then gives them a framework for taking those ideas to reality. Those who follow Phil's action plans can't help but shift their lives from 'good enough' to GREAT!"

– Jodee Bock, 'Soul' Proprietor and Catalyst for Evolution, Bock's Office Transformational Consulting

"In his 10 Ways to Make It Great! Phil Gerbyshak has pulled together a useful set of tools for those willing to take on the job of assuming responsibility for their own lives. And as he helps readers understand the tools and how to use them, his own enthusiasm provides the kind of inspiration that can keep them moving forward."

– Dick Richards, Author of Is Your Genius at Work? And OnGenius.com

"Phil Gerbyshak knows how to 'Make It Great!' in his own life. More importantly for us, he knows how to share his insights so others can learn how to do the same. By embracing just a handful of his recommended action steps, you will see a great change in your life."

– Kristen L. Gunderson, Management Systems Consultant

"Phil Gerbyshak not only gives great advice on how to 'Make It Great!,' he walks the talk. I met Phil through Young Professionals of Milwaukee and he sets a fantastic example on how those in Gen X/Y can develop their network for both professional and personal growth. Phil speaks with an honest and genuine voice in both his writing and real life—a voice that's worth listening to."

– Meghan Arnold, Senior Marketing Coordinator, MilwaukeeJobs.com

"Phil Gerbyshak's 10 Ways To Make It Great! is a wonderful pocket guide to personal transformation. This book contains no swill and no fluff. If you are looking for a simple, straight forward action plan for change, don't wait for permission to succeed, read this book now!"

— Troy Worman, writer-at-large, TroyWorman.com

"Many things are simple to understand, but not at all easy to put into action. That's why it's grand when someone like Phil Gerbyshak comes along with practical tips and exercises to show how to get to that place of ease. Don't settle for an 'ok,' 'nice,' or even 'good' life when this book, full of Phil's well-honed and practical wisdom on the topic, can give you what you need to 'Make It Great!'"

— Stacy Brice, President and Chief Visionary Officer, AssistU

"Some of us walk through life looking down, being serious, working hard, holding on to what we've earned. And some of us run and skip through life looking up, being playful, working smart, and living with an infectious generosity of spirit — Phil Gerbyshak is a great example of this second, upbeat person. His optimism, generous spirit and understanding of human nature shine through this book, providing all of us with clear action items to help us do what he's doing — making every day great!"

— Patricia Digh, author of the blog 37days

"Phil Gerbyshak reminds us of the power of choice, resolve, and passion. Curl up with 10 Ways to Make It Great! anytime you need a positive shot in the arm to live your goals. Phil oozes positive optimism and confidence. His energy and ideas can help anyone lead a more fulfilling life. Each inspiring chapter offers practical tips for living your dreams today."

— Lisa Haneberg, Management, leadership, and breakthrough author

"In 10 Ways To Make It Great! Phil Gerbyshak provides practical, straightforward steps that everyone, from age seven to seventy can use to increase what's possible in their life. If you only spent one hour per week following these action steps you will be in a very different place a few months from now. As Phil reminds us, 'life is an action sport' 10 Ways to Make It Great! can be your game plan."

— Leah Maclean, Lead Innovator, Working Solo

"Doing more, and being more is hard work! Phil Gerbyshak understands this and provides us with concrete tools we can all use on life's journey. Complete the action steps recommended in 10 Ways To Make It Great! They will support you on your personal voyage to becoming great!"

— Trevor M. Hall, Program Coordinator, Master of Arts in Servant-Leadership, Viterbo University, La Crosse

"There seems to be so much bad news in the world, and the average worker seems overworked, underappreciated, and unmotivated. Phil brings hope that things can be different; it's all up to you to 'Make It Great!' His passion and commitment come through in every page. I know that Phil lives by the principles in this book every day and wants everybody else to do the same. He is making a difference one person at a time and I admire him for that!"

– Skip Angel, CTO of Integrated Services, Inc. and author of the
Random Thoughts from a CTO blog

"I'm a big believer in approaching the world with an attitude of genuine curiosity and openness; you'll learn fun and useful things at every turn. 10 Ways to Make It Great! is a crisp collection of practical ideas that you can apply immediately. By following Phil's advice, you will learn a lot, improve yourself, and create new and interesting relationships. And you'll truly set yourself up to 'Make It Great!' in the process."

– Dwayne Melancon, author of the Genuine Curiosity blog

"Phil Gerbyshak has a simple concept for you to consider... 'Make It Great!' Phil has taken this idea and written a profound little book about it. In 10 Ways to Make It Great! Phil takes some everyday actions such as learning, dreaming, and recharging and explores their meaning and their ramifications. This is an impressive little book to keep on your desk to remind you of what is really important in life and to share that attitude with others. Pick up this book and 'Make it a Great Day!'"

– John Richardson, Author, SuccessBeginsToday.org

"Phil understands that learning is a lifelong pursuit and pushes himself out of his comfort zone to gain new insights. One of the fantastic qualities he possesses is his attention to sharing these insights where they are appropriate in life. Phil has made a tremendous impact on my life and continues to push me each and every day."

– Ryan T Schuelke, Director of Innovation, Emerging Concepts

"10 Ways To Make It Great! is a true call to action for those of us who are looking for a path to take our lives to the next level. This book will ask you the critical questions only you can answer to identify where you want to go in life, and coach you in what you need to do to take control and get there in style. Wherever you are in life, 10 Ways To Make It Great! can make a difference!"

– Sara A. Neufeldt, Product Manager, Fifth Third Bank

"10 Ways To Make It Great! shows the maturity of a young spirit. It is full of human comprehension, and acceptance of life as a colorful and complex reality. It is pregnant with intuition on the things that really matter to take charge of your life."

— *Felix Gerena, author, Three Amigos with One Message*

"10 Ways to Make It Great! is a great book! It's easy to get caught up in the day-to-day grind and overlook the importance of strong relationships, and Feed Your Friendlies does a great job of reminding us of the need to cultivate these more. 'The Four Rs' provide simple tactics that we often don't do on a regular basis, but should keep in mind and make room for on our schedule every week."

— *Jacob Cazzell, author, SuccessMinders.com*

"Phil wants you to have so much more than a nice day; he wants you to 'Make It Great!' He provides 10 ways to make your life great and outlines a variety of methods and exercises for each one. He infuses his woo, creativity, playfulness, love, gratitude and optimism into this nonlinear book. Feel free to dive into any page and make a great splash in your life. To paraphrase Tony the Tiger, this book is Grrrrrrrrrrrrrreat."

— *David Zinger, M.Ed., educator and author of DavidZinger.com and ZingeronLeadership*

"Phil Gerbyshak has written a brilliant little book. You will be able to read it in an afternoon over two glasses of wine! 10 Ways to Make It Great! is a pocket-sized manual for busy people about getting things done. I particularly like the emphasis on some of my favorite principles including:

- Don't waste time

- Find a mentor

- Work really hard and relax too

- Find time to read more

- Anything is possible

- Dreams can come true – and its not magic

- Always be optimistic

As Phil would say, you really can 'make every day a great day.' I love the simplicity of the book. If your natural style is cynical or negative, you must read this book because it will challenge your outlook. If you are a positive person you must read it because it will confirm that you are right. Your third glass of wine will taste even better after reading this book."

— *Trevor Gay, author of Simplicity is the Key*

"Fun. Practical. Effective. Committed. Phil's passion for life jumps off the pages of this book. He's not interested in us having a life that's nice, fine or even good. He wants us all to 'Make It Great!'...providing us with a map to guide us there."

– Bill Kinnon, author, TV director, Kinnon.tv

"There are a lot of people who can talk a good game. The key is taking action, not just talking. Phil's book 10 Ways To Make It Great! will have you taking action by giving you great exercises and suggestions for getting moving. I'd highly recommend it to anyone looking to live life to their true potential."

– Jon Bischke, founder, LearnOutLoud.com

"Reading 10 Ways to Make It Great! was so much fun, and I learned so much. With so many books, you finish reading them and you think to yourself 'Okay, what did I get out of that?' This book is a real get-up-and-go, get off your arse and do stuff book which is so refreshing. I can't wait to read the sequel!"

– Ruben Schade, host of the Rubenerd Variety Show

"There are some people who view the world, well, differently. They see life as an active sport – and every single day as an opportunity for being positive, proactive – and engaged. Fortunately for all of us, one of those people is Phil Gerbyshak. Refreshing, positive and always there with a smile, Phil has put together and shared 10 steps of meaningful advice for his mantra of 'Make It Great!' Lots of people talk about 'feel-good' movies and books. The problem? They make you feel good, but only temporarily. Few people concentrate on a practical approach on HOW to feel good—or even better, how to 'make it great.' Until now. Put Phil Gerbyshak's 10 Ways to Make It Great! among the most practical approaches to creating a positive and optimistic perspective on life on the journey to making 'it' great. I dare you to read Phil's 10 Ways to Make It Great! and not walk away with a smile on your face, a renewed passion for life, and an improved appreciation for all things POSITIVE."

– Skip Reardon, Director of Marketing, Six Disciplines Corporation,
and author of Be Excellent™

"Warning: Reading this book could change the rest of your life! If you do not know Phil Gerbyshak yet, you should! The idea of 'Make It Great!' is so powerful because it is so elegant and simple. This volume is not about PMA on steroids, instead, it contain a clear methodology for designing an amazing life with true significance. Phil's underlying message that individual excellence starts with a personal choice is 100% correct."

– Thom Quinn, philosopher-at-large, ThomQuinn.com

CONTENTS

Phil Gerbyshak

Foreword to 10 Ways to Make It Great!

Having worked in the Human Resources field for over 15 years, I have been exposed to many different people and their styles. I have also experienced their "blocks" in this world; the things that keep people from achieving greatness and from reaching their goals. Unfortunately, most people are quite content to just "go through the motions" and let life happen TO them. I have met very few people that make things happen FOR them. Phil Gerbyshak is definitely the latter.

I gained the clarity Phil speaks of after the death of my father. He was a person who had wonderful creative ideas and aspired to do many things; travel the globe, write a book, visit the great art museums of the world. The problem was that he only talked about doing these things. For whatever reason, he never acted upon them and then when he contracted cancer, he found himself at the end of his life with many regrets. I have since created that life list of things to do before I die; I've published a book; I've visited the great art museums of the world; I continue to travel the globe. Some of those things I do for him and some I do for myself.

After reading this book, you will think that Phil's message sounds so simple. There is a good reason for that…IT IS! Only you can choose how you will react to situations and only you can decide what you want your future to be. If you aren't happy with your current situation, you have a couple of options. The first option is to complain about it and just let it continue. I don't know about you, but that doesn't sound like a good option to me. The second option is to just let it continue and suffer in silence. Again… not a good option in my book. The third option is to change it. Sometimes taking that leap is scary. Trust me…I've done it many times and it isn't always easy, but it is always worth it. Don't be afraid of failure; it is the basis for a lot of great learning!

The 10 tips in this book outline a great framework for success. Some people just wait for success to find them. I'm sure if you read any books about those in this world we consider very successful, you will find that many sacrificed a great deal or overcame major obstacles; success just didn't happen to them. If you are committed to making changes in how you view the world and your mission in it, you certainly have what it takes to "Make It Great!"

Jackie Valent MSHR, SPHR
Human Resources Executive
Author, *Stinky the Bulldog*

1

Don't Settle For Nice...

Life is an active sport. It's one you have to take some control of if you want it to be good, and more control of if you want it to be great. Granted, there are many things that may be out of your control for one reason or another. Early in my life, I realized the only thing I can control is my attitude. Only I can truly Make It Great! So I've decided to take it upon myself to always try to be positive, even when things are less than desirable. When you ask me how I'm doing, I am great! Really, I am!

Make It Great!

Make It Great! means it's my choice, which means it's your choice too. Whether you actually have a good day or a not so good day is not the important thing; what's important is how you choose to deal with the things that each day brings. Each encounter presents you with an opportunity to either let it pass by, or tackle it head on and truly Make It Great!

Why not just "Have a Nice Day?"

Make It Great! means I am in charge of, and taking charge of, my actions, and reactions, to my life. I am making it Great! If you "have a nice day," you are content to let whatever happens, happen, and you are allowing life to have control over you. Doing so is fine, if you just want to have a NICE day! If you're reading this, I'm betting you want to Make It Great! so that's what we'll do.

How to Use This Book

Each chapter in this book will have one or more action steps for you to take to Make It Great! I recommend you focus on one chapter at a time, think about it, and take the action steps suggested. Write down what kind of difference those actions make in your life.

This book is not meant to be linear, so feel free to jump around to whatever chapter grabs your attention, and come back to the other chapters later. Seize the day, take charge of the opportunities that come your way, and Make It Great!

My Goal with 10 Ways To Make It Great!

My goal is to pack the rest of this book full of little things you can do to take control of your life and Make It Great! If you complete the recommended action steps I suggest at the end of each chapter, you will be making it great!

If you do, I'd love to hear about your success stories. You are welcome to contact me at anytime during your personal journey with 10 Ways To Make It Great! by e-mailing me at philg@makeitgreat.org

Without further ado, let the journey begin!

1.

Begin at the End and Work Toward Today

What would you change if you knew you had only one day left to live? Would you spend more time at work, pouring over budget figures, and trying to figure out how you were going to make this quarter's numbers? Would you read just one more e-mail from a complaining co-worker? Would you check your voicemail one last time? What would your obituary say about your life?

If you're like me, I'd bet you wouldn't do anything work-related. In fact, I bet you would see if there was any way to extend that one day into six months or more, because there is so much you have yet to accomplish. Maybe you would vow to make a difference in your family, with your friends, in your community, or somewhere else in the world. Maybe you'd see if you could sky dive, climb Pike's Peak, or snorkel the Great Barrier Reef.

If you knew when the end was, I'd guess you would do all those things you've been meaning to do, but just never had the time to do. What's stopping you from doing them now?

ACTION STEP 1:

Write your obituary as though today were your last day. Be honest! Write what you really think people will remember about you.

Some things you might want to include are:

- Who is mourning you?
- What difference did you make in the lives of those around you?
- How is the world a better place because of what you did?

_____

_____

_____

_____

_____

_____

_____

_____

_____

_____

_____

_____

ACTION STEP 2:

Now, take out a pen and paper and make a list of what you'd like to do if you were to die tomorrow. What is included? What are you doing right now that you need to stop doing? Re-write your obituary now based on what you'd rather be remembered for.

After you have this clarity, think about what will you do to Make It Great! on a daily basis, and start doing it right away!

_____

_____

_____

_____

_____

_____

_____

_____

_____

_____

_____

_____

_____

_____

ACTION STEP 3:

What is the one thing you can you do to Make It Great! right now? Write what that one thing is and a date for when you will take action on that item to Make It Great!

My one thing is:

_____

_____

_____

_____

_____

_____

_____

_____

_____

_____

_____

_____

_____

_____

_____

2.

Learn About Yourself as Much as Possible

On my personal journey to Make It Great! I have learned a great deal of information about myself. No, not that my favorite color is Carolina blue, or that I enjoy piña coladas and getting caught in the rain. Not those kinds of things. I've learned many useful things about myself which help me be more energized, and which have allowed me to stop giving away my energy to less productive avenues.

One of the first things I did was take an online assessment called the Clifton StrengthsFinder™[1], offered by the Gallup organization. The test allows you to discover your five key themes, or areas of personal strength. I discovered that my key themes are:

* Ideation – The strength of ideation means I am fascinated by new ideas, especially when I can discover an elegantly simple way to explain why things are the way they are. That's why this book has been such fun for me to write, and is so wonderful for me to share with you.

* Woo –Woo stands for Winning Others Over, which means I enjoy meeting new people and getting them to like me.

* Maximizer –Maximizer means I enjoy taking something that is already strong, and turning it into something superb. It's why I enjoy learning about myself,

especially my strengths, and why I feel it's so critical that you learn as much about yourself as possible. This chapter is all about me helping you maximize your life.

- Relator – Interestingly, my relator qualities pulls me close to people I already know. I get a great deal of pleasure and strength from being around my closest friends. Anyone who knows me knows this is true.

- Strategic – This strength is what allows me to see patterns where others see only complexity. My strategic strength has been very helpful for me when working in the information technology community, as a teacher, and in the financial sector.

Having the "Woo" strength as so much of my character, I also took an inter-personal communications assessment, so I could understand how I communicate and how I could become a better communicator with others. I learned I am a driver-expressive, which means I like to express myself by using any means necessary, and often will talk more than anyone else in the room. I also learned that I like to be in control of the situation at hand, and about how this part of my nature can determine my effectiveness in communicating well.

Some of the tests available for learning about your interpersonal communication style include DiSC[2], the Keirsey Temperament Sorter[3], and the Platinum Rule Behavioral Style Assessment.[4]

Another self-awareness tool that is available, for a small price, is an online Myers Briggs ®[5] test. Taking this test, I found out I am an ENFP (Extraverted Intuitive Feeling Perceiving guy), and that my wife is just the opposite of me.

According to the MBTI ®[6], my four quadrants are:

Extraverted – I'm outgoing, and enjoy talking with people and get energized by groups of people, and I enjoy energizing others. This trait has served me well as a manager, leader, teacher, and a teammate.

Intuitive – I act based on what's in my gut more than sensing to see what might be there. This is helpful for me when I get into unfamiliar territory, when I have no facts to back up my decisions, and must act based on what I "feel" is right.

Feeling – I make decisions often based on how people feel, and try to make the best decision for all parties involved.

Perceiving – I prefer a more flexible and spontaneous life, and don't get bogged down in the details. It's fun to be this flexible, but it's hard because many people aren't this way and don't understand why I am the way that I am. I see this happen often when I agree to do something before I know all the details, just because I trust the person who asked me or because it "sounds like fun."

Taking these three tests has really helped me understand what makes me tick. The more you know about yourself, the more you can take that knowledge to focus on your strengths, and the easier it is to spot those that can help you Make It Great! and fill in your weaknesses. Self-knowledge helps you compensate for your weaknesses, and enables you to surround yourself with those that are complementary to you. It's why diversity of thought is so important. If I had 10 people on my team, just like me, I'd be in trouble.

Instead, I hire people who are different from me, and we work together very well.

ACTION STEP 4:

Complete the free MBTI ® sample self-assessment on my website or one of the other two self-assessments mentioned in the chapter. Note your results, and the reactions to those results, below. Ask your friends, family, and co-workers what they think of your results, and see if they agree. Lastly, recognize that you can't be good at everything, so focus on what you are good at and use your strengths to Make It Great!

Tests/Assessments I Want to Take:

Results of my tests:

My reactions to my results:

_____

_____

_____

_____

_____

_____

_____

_____

_____

_____

_____

_____

_____

_____

_____

_____

_____

Others' reactions to my results:

_____

_____

_____

_____

_____

_____

_____

_____

_____

_____

_____

_____

_____

_____

_____

_____

_____

_____

Phil Gerbyshak

3.

Use the 80/20 Rule As A Key to Your Success

Perhaps you've heard of the 80/20 rule but don't know where it came from or how it was adapted. Allow me to give a bit of background on the 80/20 rule before I jump into how you can put it to work for you.

In 1906, Italian economist Vilfredo Pareto[7] came up with a mathematical principle to describe the distribution of wealth in his country. He found that 20% of the people had 80% of Italy's wealth.

In the late 1940s, a quality management guru by the name of Dr. Joseph Juran[8] observed a theory of the "vital few" and the "trivial many" and incorrectly attributed this to Pareto, thus the "Pareto Principle" was named and the "80/20 rule" became the common phrase to describe how to be more effective

Eighty-twenty (80-20) defined[9]:

A term referring to the Pareto[7] principle, which was first defined by J. M. Juran in 1950. The principle suggests most effects come from relatively few causes; that is, 80% of the effects come from 20% of the possible causes.

"The Vital Few" are the 20% that produce 80% of the outcome. When you Make It Great!, you put yourself in position to be one of these "Vital Few" that create 80% of the outcomes.

Focusing on these vital few in your life can make a huge

difference in the accomplishments you can make in your life. Everyone is good at a few things, so make your vital few, great.

As an example, let's assume you have a 10-item To Do list. Chances are you'll find that there are two things on your list that have more value than the other eight things combined. These are the two things that absolutely must be done for the day, and according to the Pareto Principle, the other 80% on your list can be given to someone else to do, planned for another day, or ignored altogether without minimizing your overall effectiveness.

By accomplishing these two items, you will do more than you ever thought possible. Chances are these two things are often the hardest things on your list. Some would say that doing something is better than doing nothing. I argue that doing the eight little things is a lot like doing nothing, because they're little things that don't amount to much. Doing the two big things will give you the confidence you need to do even bigger things. Then you'll achieve more, believe in yourself more, thus doing even bigger things, and you will have the effect of creating momentum with consistent effort in the right direction is now in your favor.

Do those difficult, valuable things, and watch your achievements go through the roof. Of course, you can always focus on the trivial few actions and focus on just getting any old thing done to tick off many items on that to-do list. But this will never really allow you to get ahead. It's really up to you, and I hope you'll choose to Make It Great! and make every effort count.

ACTION STEP 5:

Determine the really important items (20%) in your life, family, and career are. Spend more time on these "vital few" things, and less time on everything else (80%) and you will Make It Great! in no time!

Remember: 80% of your results will come from 20% of your actions, so try to beef up the 80% of your results to even greater heights!

What's on Your "To-Do" List?

_____

_____

_____

_____

_____

_____

_____

_____

_____

_____

_____

_____

_____

_____

_____

_____

_____

_____

Review your "to-do" list from the previous page

What are the two or three things you can do RIGHT NOW that will have the biggest impact on you achieving your goals? Write them below, and get started on these items TODAY!

_____

_____

_____

_____

_____

_____

_____

_____

_____

_____

_____

_____

_____

_____

4.
Never Stop Learning!

One of the easiest ways to ensure you Make It Great! is to never stop learning. "I'll stop learning when I'm dead!" is my motto. One of the richest sources for learning available to you, are books.

Most adults never read another book – for business or pleasure - after they graduate from high school. Jerrold Jenkins of the Jenkins Group[10] reports the following shocking statistics:

- 33% of high school graduates will never read another book for the rest of their lives.

- 58% of the total US adult population has never read another book since high school.

- 42% of college graduates will never read another book after college.

- 80% of US families did not buy or read a book last year.

- 70% of US adults have not been in a bookstore in the last five years.

- 57% of new books are not read to completion.

That's a powerful thing to understand: Most adults never read another book after they graduate high school, for business or pleasure. Not a single book. How far ahead could you get if you read a book a week, a book a month, or even just a book a year? Reading books can help keep your mind sharp.

The biggest reason given for not reading? "I don't have time!" So how can you possibly fit in the time to read a book a week? The easiest, most painless way to "read" a book a week (or a month) is to listen to them via MP3 or on CD, in your car, or when you exercise.

Where can you get these audio books? These days, almost every book worth reading (this one will be on audio soon too) is on audio CD. You can get audio CDs at your public library, at your local bookseller or at various places online.

"But I don't have time to listen to an MP3 player, or to exercise, and my kids always want me to spend time with them. Then how do I listen to these books?" Easy – you listen to them in your car on your way back and forth to work, to school, to wherever you are going. As Zig Ziglar says, "Your car is your university!" I couldn't agree more.

Here are 15 of my favorite non-fiction recommendations to help you get started:

All Marketers are Liars – Seth Godin
Pitch Like a Girl - Ronna Lichtenberg
Between Trapezes - Gail Blanke
Death By Meeting – Patrick Lencioni
First Things First – Stephen R. Covey

How to Win Friends and Influence People – Dale Carnegie
Leadership is an Art – Max Depree
Love is the Killer App – Tim Sanders
Never Eat Alone – Keith Ferrazzi
The Art of the Start – Guy Kawasaki
The Best Year of Your Life - Debbie Ford
The Fred Factor – Mark Sanborn
The Power of Positive Thinking – Norman Vincent Peale
Think and Grow Rich – Napoleon Hill
Turning to One Another - Margaret Wheatley

The benefits of lifelong learning are endless. Think of how much further ahead you could be with your life's goals if you read a book a week? If even an hour a day were devoted to reading, you could definitely achieve this, and those extra 20 or more books a year could easily make you an expert on whatever you wanted to be an expert in. Then, once you're an expert, you'll make more money, have more time and be more knowledgeable so you can devote your efforts to those things you really want to do — the 20 that gets you the 80 to Make It Great!

Six Tips for Easy Lifelong Learning

Reading or listening to books is just one way to learn. Below are six of my other favorite tips.

1. Join a professional organization and use their training outlets - You may already be part of an organization like Toastmasters, a local writer's workshop group, or

something else of that nature. There are a wealth of other organizations out there to suit your interests and needs. If you're not sure, ask around. You'll be surprised to find out which organizations the people around you are affiliated with, and you can find out if the organization is worth your time before you even get started.

2. Pursue a degree - Perhaps starting or completing an undergraduate degree can help you Make It Great! by increasing your personal credibility. For some, an advanced degree like an MBA or Master's degree in a particular field may be what you need to advance your career path or to stay sharp in your current job. There are a number of programs available to you - some are online, some are taught in the traditional class room setting, and some blend the two. Most colleges offer flexible schedules and have offerings that will fit into your schedule.

3. Get Certified - An industry-specific certification is required to stay current in many jobs. Just like a traditional college, you can do self-paced study or take a class online to get the certification you need to move up. Check with your employer: Many companies offer tuition reimbursement for certification programs, and will provide sources for you to choose from.

4. Take advantage of your company's training offerings - Many larger companies offer in-house training to

associates. What have you got to lose by talking to your manager, supervisor, or HR department about the classes that are available to you? If you're fortunate, you'll get a few different ideas. Doing training in what you're already skilled in can help take your skills from very good, to great! Often, companies will happily pay for training that related directly to your job, you just have to find the connection.

5. Visit a website that's topic-specific to what you want to learn. - If you're looking for a good book or for that perfect website, use a search engine like Google.com, MSN.com, or Yahoo.com and enter a few key words about a topic you are interested in learning more about. The web is full of information that can help you learn more about what you need to know. Many authors and other experts freely give away a sampling (or more) of their information on their website or on their blog. At the very least, they'll share their favorite resources and offer you some useful links.

6. Find a mentor - My sixth tip is something you can do at anytime. Seek someone in your company with whom you are comfortable asking questions. Buy them lunch and pick their brain. Or look online and e-mail an expert. You'd be surprised at how many people are willing to help, if you'll just ask them. Maybe they'll even become a formal mentor of yours and be willing to invest some of their time in helping you advance your career and your life.

ACTION STEP 6:

If you don't already have one, go get a library card right now. Pick a topic that will help you make your life and/or your career great, and make it one of your goals to read at least a book a month, every month, for the next year. Some possible topics might include how to write more effectively, ways to improve your written or verbal communication skills, how to understand more about people, the various learning styles, or anything else that you think you need to learn. Repeat this practice each year until you know everything about that topic, then change topics and do it again!

Send an e-mail to philg@makeitgreat.org if you'd like a personal book recommendation or two.

_____

_____

_____

_____

_____

_____

_____

_____

Two topics I am interested in are:

Books or resources I will use to learn about my top two topics:

_____

_____

_____

_____

_____

_____

_____

_____

_____

_____

_____

_____

_____

_____

Phil Gerbyshak

5.

Surround Yourself With Those Who Can Help You

"The answer is always no…unless you ask."
- Unknown

Whatever job you might hold, this quote is an incredibly true statement. If you don't ask someone for help, they most likely won't help you. Chances are they won't even know you need help. I think most people like to help others. By asking, you're giving them a chance to help you Make It Great! and be your hero.

So I say ask away, and do not be concerned if you may never be able to repay their kindness and compassion. Ask anyway, for you can pay it forward and help someone else who may not be able to repay you.

"It's not what you know, it's who you know, that's important."
- Unknown

I'm sure you've heard this saying a thousand times before, but let me change this slightly to tell you what's important now: "It's not what you know, it's who knows you that's important."

Remember the key part of this new way of thinking: you may feel you "know" people, but if those people don't "know" you, what kind of relationship is that? How can they help you if they don't know you?

I would argue that this is not a relationship at all, rather something you got just by grabbing someone's business card and not really taking the time to get to know them. People love to talk about themselves, and there are many who say that people have a more favorable impression of you when you ask them questions about themselves.

Encourage people to tell you how they're really doing by asking open-ended questions. The next chapter will help you learn more about the power of open-ended questions.

Don't answer others' questions to you with the adjective "fine." Think of "fine" as the acronym "Feelings I'm Not Expressing." Is that really what you're trying to get across to people, that you're hiding your feelings? Be open, be honest, and just let it be!

So get out there, ask questions, and get to know people. Let people get to know you!

CAUTION: *You just might meet someone you can call your friend!*

ACTION STEP 7:

If you don't have personal business cards, make some on your home computer. A quick and easy business card can be made with a headshot of you on one side of the card, combined with all of your contact information on the other side of the card. Include your personal mantra or favorite quote if you have one, or any other point of interest that might be a conversation starter.

ACTION STEP 8:

Now that you have your business cards, use them frequently and effectively. Put 10 cards in your pocket every time you leave the house. Put 10 cards in your car, put 10 in your briefcase or book-bag, and put three or four in your wallet. You never know when you're going to get an opportunity to meet someone who can help you or who you can help.

ACTION STEP 9:

Join an organization related to your current career, or if you want to make a career switch soon, join an organization that's related to the career you want to be in. Make it a point to attend every meeting for the next six months, and to meet at least three new people at each meeting. Exchange business cards, do breakfast, lunch, dinner or coffee with these new people, and pick their brain about how they got good at their current position, and if they could help you learn more. Most people want to help, you just need to ask!

ACTION STEP 10:

Think about your three best friends and find out what's really going on in their life. Don't take "fine" for an answer. Challenge them to Make It Great! by sharing their struggles and joys with you. Invest time in them and share your struggles and joys with them after they have shared with you. Together, you can find the answers that can help each of you Make It Great!

6.
Feed Your Friendlies

What do I mean by feed your friendlies? I mean that in order to Make It Great! you absolutely must make the time to nourish those relationships that give you the most energy, provide you with insight, and are good for you, whenever and as often as possible. These friendlies could be folks you know intimately well, like family, your best friends, or a co-worker. They could be someone you met once who made an impact on you, like a great author, writer, speaker, or someone you met online at a website of like-minded thinkers.

You also need to know why these people are your friendlies, how you can help them, and how they can help you.

Ask Open-Ended Questions

Learning to know more about your friendlies can be done by starting with a few open-ended questions. An open-ended question is a question that cannot be answered with a simple yes or no. They are open-ended because they offer people the opportunity to tell a story. You never know when you'll get an opportunity to get to know someone more, so always have a few open-ended questions ready to ask.

Below are a few sample open-ended questions:

- Tell me more about (insert whatever someone just mentioned that you have a genuine interest in).

- How did that make you feel?

- Share with me your greatest joy in life

- What does that mean to you?

- Tell me about the best vacation you've ever taken.

ACTION STEP 11:

Determine who your friendlies are; write a list of names here of those you would sincerely enjoy spending more time with.

My Friendlies Are:

_____

_____

_____

_____

_____

_____

_____

_____

_____

_____

_____

_____

_____

ACTION STEP 12:

Schedule time with your friendlies writing specific dates below for the next six months. Choose your venue (a telephone call or email, coffee or lunch, some other event you could invite them to.)

_____

_____

_____

_____

_____

_____

_____

_____

_____

_____

_____

_____

_____

_____

_____

_____

7.

Dream Big Dreams, Do Big Things!

How can dreams help you do more and be more than you ever thought possible? How can you make your dreams a more powerful force in your life?

I'll begin with the second question first, making dreams a more powerful part of your life. The first step in making dreams powerful is to go to bed thinking about that which you want to dream about. That means turning off the TV and tuning into something else that you want to dream about. If you want to dream about accomplishing more in life, re-read your goals before you fall asleep. If you haven't already written down your goals, take 10 minutes and write one down tonight before you go to sleep, and tomorrow night, another one, and the next night another one, until you have all the goals you want to achieve written down. You can go low-tech with a notebook or 3x5 index cards, or high tech and type them on your computer and print them off on full sheets of paper. It doesn't much matter; just write those things down somewhere you can refer to them frequently.

Having proactively channeled dreams can help you do more and be more than you ever thought possible. The more you think about something, consciously or unconsciously, the more you find ways to accomplish those thoughts. If your goal is to make $250,000 per year, and you write it down, and re-read it before bed, your mind will automatically think of new ways for you to make more money.

Now to the best part: how to become a better dreamer. The first thing you can do to become a dreamer is to set up a dream room, a room or place you can go to get away from it all and just think. This could be outside, under a favorite tree, in your basement, or anywhere that you have the freedom to dream! Bring along a notebook, a few pens and pencils, and maybe a music playing device. A tape recorder can be used to record your thoughts as they come to you. No matter where this is, make it a special place, and go there whenever you need to dream. Make it special, and you'll Make It Great!

The next thing is to learn as shared with you in the section on Lifelong Learning; always learn more about whatever it is you're passionate about, whatever it is you want to dream about. I encourage you to go back and re-read Chapter Four, Never Stop Learning!

Go to the library and get all the books you can get about the topic, and read them. Take them to your dream room with you, and make notes on what you read, and use these to help clarify your goals.

Last, and possibly most important, be persistent. You won't be a great dreamer right away. It will take time, and that's okay. In fact, that's more than okay, that's normal.

ACTION STEP 13:

Dream a BIG dream, and write it down. Use descriptive words to make your dream real to you! This book was the result of one of my big dreams!

My first BIG dream is:

_____

_____

_____

_____

_____

_____

_____

_____

_____

_____

_____

_____

_____

ACTION STEP 14:

Buy a few magazines, draw a few pictures, or search the Internet for graphics that show your dreams manifested. Create a collage, and hang in somewhere you can see it frequently.

ACTION STEP 15:

Share your dream with two people you know will support your dreams. Ask them to check in with you in 30 days, 90 days, six months, and then ever year until your dream is achieved to your satisfaction. This accountability circle is key to achieving your dreams, because the more supportive people you have around you, the more your dream is, and the faster it will become reality.

ACTION STEP 16:

Repeat action steps 14 and 15 until you've achieved everything you want to achieve in your life.

8.

Work Hard Now...Or Work Hard Forever!

If I work hard now, I invest whatever time it takes to get my job done effectively and efficiently, and a bit more. For me, working harder is often above-and-beyond the 40 hours I am paid to work. If I work hard now, I'm able to get ahead of others who work just hard enough to get by and do what they do. By working hard now, I can avoid having to work hard later.

Working hard does not mean that you need work more than 40 hours per week. It means that you must be productive in the 40 hours you do work each week, and squeeze as much out of the hours, minutes and seconds expected of you every day. Give each time period everything you've got, and you will be far more productive than the person who waits 20 years to start working hard.

By working hard now, I am also setting the table for my future successes by investing the time right now to do what I need to do to be successful, to get my name out there so people view me as an advocate for them, and to prove that I am willing to pay the price for success.

The harder I work now, the less hard I'll have to work later. On the other hand, if I choose to be one who just gets by, then I'll have to work hard forever and keep doing "just enough." I'm sure you know plenty of people who do this, and then they wonder why they never get ahead in their career or in their personal life. For me, I prefer to work hard now, put in my time, and rise to the top.

Think about the difference between getting paid for completing a job or responsibility, and contrast that with the job where you only get paid for the hours you work. I enjoy getting paid a wage based on my output, as it drives me on to produce more. With an hourly employee attitude, one can feel less invested in what's going on, because we tend to merely "punch the clock."

So it's your choice. Work hard now to produce something substantial and be noticed for your work so you can rightfully move into something that rewards you more. Or, work hard forever, punching the clock of life and never finding true fulfillment or rewards in what you do.

ACTION STEP 17:

Commit to working hard now. Put an extra five hours every week toward making your career great! This doesn't necessarily mean five additional hours "on the job." This could be five hours reading a book or magazine related to your current vocation or future vocation, attending an organization of like-minded individuals, or taking a class on a topic you need to know to take your life to the next level. Repeat this every week for at least a year, and write down below the changes you've seen in your life because of this.

_____

_____

_____

_____

_____

_____

_____

_____

_____

_____

ACTION STEP 18:

Take an hour write now to review the previous action steps you've taken from this book. If you haven't done any yet, commit to doing at least 1 this week. Complete one action step a week, or every two weeks, and charge your results below.List other actions I will take to work harder now:

_____

_____

_____

_____

_____

_____

_____

_____

_____

_____

_____

_____

_____

9.

Recharge Your Batteries

One of the things that so many people neglect as a key with which they can Make It Great! is re-charging their batteries. By this, I mean that they run hot for so long and ultimately get burned out. I have been guilty of this, and have stopped just short of completing some of my goals because I started out too fast. Keeping in mind that life is a marathon, not a sprint is helpful, but there are more than self-affirmations to help you recharge and rejuvenate.

There are Four R's that I've found help me Make It Great!

Rest - This is one of the hardest things for me to do. I find that I don't need a ton of sleep every single night, but four out of seven nights, I really need my seven to eight hours of sleep to feel completely refreshed and recharged. Your mileage may vary, but seven to eight hours should be enough according to many experts.

One thing that I find really hurts me is oversleeping to try to catch up. These long power snoozes don't help, and in fact, they end up making me more tired than before. I've found that being consistent with getting seven to eight hours of sleep a night is much better for me. You'll find your sweet spot, and once you do, do everything you can to stay in it!

Originally reported in the April 25, 2003 issue of Psychology Today[11], it was noted "You cannot make up for lost sleep in only one day." If you didn't get enough sleep for the past week, take the next week or so to go to bed earlier than usual, and get up at your usual time. You'll eventually get back in the groove, but it will take time. The best advice is to not fall behind if at all possible.

Reflect - I find that taking the time to reflect on what's happening in my life every few days helps me keep things in perspective and stops negative thoughts before they get out of control. Contrary to what some may think, my life is not perfect; I have my bad days too. I make time to think about why they were bad days, and make sure I keep those variables out of my life as much as I can. Of course some days are easier than others, but taking the time to reflect helps me understand how I'm feeling, and hopefully why I'm feeling that way. It takes practice, to be sure, however it's worth it!

Read - I read as much as I can and include reflection time. You don't have to read a novel to get away; find a blog you enjoy, an online newsletter that pumps you up, or just an old e-mail from a friend. Think about the words and really immerse yourself in whatever you're reading. It will help you de-stress and re-charge.

Relax - We all relax differently, some by reading, some by reflecting, some by resting, and some by doing something altogether different. Perhaps you have an activity like prayer, meditation or yoga that helps you relax. Or maybe there's a favorite place you can go that immediately calms you down. Whatever or wherever that is, do it or get there NOW!

ACTION STEP 16:

Schedule time for your Four R's this week.

Rest this week by going to bed 30 minutes early. In the morning, write down how you feel below.

_____

_____

_____

_____

_____

_____

_____

_____

_____

_____

_____

_____

_____

_____

_____

Reflect 15-30 minutes on how your day went immediately before you go to bed. Did you get what you wanted done?

Do you know what needs to be done to Make It Great! tomorrow?

_____

_____

_____

_____

_____

_____

_____

_____

_____

_____

_____

_____

_____

_____

_____

Read Something

Pick up a new magazine, newspaper, or journal that you've been wanting to read, or do an Internet search on an interesting new topic. Set a goal to read about this new topic 3-5 times per week for an entire month. Compile the articles you found interesting in a special folder. At the end of the month, review the articles you read and write a page or two about what you found especially interesting, or just note the names and authors of the articles you enjoyed. Continue doing this until you've run out of things that interest you, then start over at the beginning of your folders. Soon, you'll have your very own library of useful information you can share with family and friends.Relax this upcoming weekend by getting up at the same time you do during the week and making yourself a nice cup of coffee or tea before everyone else is awake.

10.

Finish What You Start...

Some people would argue that the toughest part of any project is getting started. I feel just the opposite, that it's actually hardest to complete something. Why, you ask? Because there's a thrill I get when I start something new. It's exciting to say that I'm starting on a new goal. It's fun to go buy a new pair of running shoes, a few new t-shirts, some new shorts, and some clean socks. But then I don't run, or I don't run for very long. I actually enjoy the process of setting goals, planning to achieve some great things, but then I fade out and don't achieve them.

...and Just Get Started!

OK, so maybe you have trouble getting started. If you've made it through the book, and still aren't sure where to begin with the action steps and suggestions I've made, I encourage you to just do SOMETHING, ANYTHING, and see what happens naturally. Getting started can be just as hard as finishing for some, so just dive in and do it!

You can do almost anything in the world that you want to, if only you commit yourself to it, practice it perfectly, and continue working on it until you're the best in the world.

ACTION STEP 17:

Set more goals!

Set MORE goals? How will this help you start, or finish more, as you now have more to start, and finish, than before? This works because the more goals you set, the more practice you get setting goals, the more practice you'll get finishing goals, and the easier it gets to finish even more goals.

The key is the type of goals you set. Set those big goals for things that scare you, then break them up into manageable yearly parts. Then break them into quarterly parts, and then into monthly parts. Take it further and break them into weekly parts, and then into daily parts. Finally identify the tasks that you can accomplish to get you going in the right direction. Feel the exhilaration of completing those tasks and achieving these smaller goals, and watch them lead to bigger, better, greater achievements in your life.

ACTION STEP 18:

Celebrate in the process of achieving more. As you take steps to achieving your goals, celebrate the milestone accomplishments when you are 20 percent, 50 percent, 80 percent, 90 percent, and, of course, 100 percent complete. These are important milestones that when celebrated, can renew your energy and encourage you to persevere through the tough times. Don't be fooled, there will be tough times. But you can make it through!

ACTION STEP 19:

Time audit your past week so you begin to recognize the successes you had, what you DID get started and what you DID complete, and can analyze the patterns on when you are successful during the week, and compare that to when you aren't.

ACTION STEP 20:

Reward yourself appropriately for your successes. When you start something big, often you will say the goal itself is enough of a reward. This is simply not true. Find something that you want, put it out there, and aim for it. Often the better the reward, the harder you will press. But don't give yourself the prize for 90 percent complete. Make sure you nail it and get it 100 percent complete. A reward is something you give yourself for a job well done, or for achieving a worthwhile goal. For a weight loss goal, you might want to reward yourself with a new suit, a nice pair of shoes, or a nice dinner with a special someone at a restaurant you've wanted to try. For other goals, a new DVD, music CD, or book you've been wanting can be a great reward. Choose something that's meaningful for you and specific enough to your goal so when you see it, you know how you got it.

Phil Gerbyshak

About Phil Gerbyshak

Phil Gerbyshak is a motivational speaker and writer who challenges each individual whose life he touches to find their inner greatness. He believes that each person can unleash the power within by improving their attitude, setting goals and changing their way of thinking. His mantra, "Make it Great!" is not just a statement, but a way of life, and he believes it can be everyone's.

Phil enjoys exploring innovative ways to lead and motivate others while building deep and meaningful relationships with a diverse group of people. It's that gratification that drives him in his current role as a Help Desk Manager for a regional financial services firm. He is also President Elect for the Professional Help Desk Association, an organization that provides support professionals with regular opportunities to meet and share ideas and solutions to common challenges. A self-proclaimed life-long learner, Phil earned his bachelors' degree from Lakeland College and was a Communications Technician in the United States Navy for four years.

An internationally syndicated writer, Phil is an expert author at EzineArticles.com, contributing author to Synergy Weblog, 100 Bloggers, and a writer for MilwaukeeJobs.com. His first masterpiece, a book titled 10 Ways to Make it Grea!t was published in May of 2006.

Phil is active in several of Milwaukee's organizations

including Young Professionals of Milwaukee and Cream City Communicators. He diligently promotes the Milwaukee Art Museum and the Urban Ecology Center, two venues he feels are unlike any others. Phil resides in Milwaukee where he looks to start a family with his wife, Kim. They are members of Church in the City, a place Phil invites everyone to visit should they have the chance.

MakeItGreat.org, Phil's primary Web site, is updated frequently with motivational articles and links to help you "Make it Great!" He extends everyone the same courtesy, "If there's ever anything I can do for you, please ask and if I can do it, I will!"

EPILOGUE

Thanks again for joining me on this journey. I hope you've been able to find some new ways to Make It Great! for you! If I can ever be of assistance to you or someone you know, please contact me at philg@makeitgreat.org

I hope you enjoyed this book. If you'd like to find any of my other tools referenced in this book, head over to my website at http://10waystomakeitgreat.com

Once you're on my website, you are welcome to Make It Great! by signing up for my FREE weekly newsletter.

Immediately after signing up, I'll send you an 11th tip to Make It Great!, and then each week, you'll enjoy the weekly Make It Great! Gazette. I realize your privacy is important to you: Your e-mail is 100% safe with me, for I share my list with nobody. You will not be spammed.

Until we meet in person, thank you for choosing to Make It Great!

Phil Gerbyshak

Phil Gerbyshak

Additional Resources

Book Site

10WaystoMakeItGreat.com is the site dedicated to this book. On the site, you'll find some stories about how others like you have made it great, business card templates, tools to help you create a mantra, and much more!

Sign up for the Make It Great! Gazette

Head over to 10waystomakeitgreat.com to sign up for my free weekly newsletter, packed full of tips and tricks on how you can Make It Great!, plus additional resources, book reviews, stories, and much more.

Make It Great! Blog

MakeItGreat.org is my blog, featuring near daily posts about what's going on in the world of leadership, management, business, technology, and much more. Links to my book reviews, newsletters I subscribe to which help motivate me, some of my favorite other authors and writers, and much more, all free for the taking.

Phil Gerbyshak

End Notes

1. http://gmj.gallup.com/book_center/strengthsfinder/

2. http://www.discprofile.com/

3. http://keirsey.com/matrix.html

4. http://www.platinumrule.com/free-assessment.asp

5. http://www.myersbriggs.org/

6. http://www.myersbriggs.org/my%5Fmbti%5Fpersonality%5Ftype/
   mbti%5Fbasics/

7. http://en.wikipedia.org/wiki/Pareto_principle/

8. http://www.juran.com/

9. http://en.wikipedia.org/wiki/80-20_rule

10. http://www.jenkinsgroup.com

11. http://www.psychologytoday.com/articles/pto-20030425-000002.html

Phil Gerbyshak

2216878

Made in the USA